“Dedicated t
gave me lov

Sunny Bindra

Sunny Bindra is a management consultant, writer and teacher. He works with directors and chief executives in leading Kenyan companies, helping them develop creative strategic thinking. His experience has spanned Africa, the United Kingdom and Asia Pacific.

Sunny is a weekly columnist on *The Sunday Nation*, East Africa's highest-circulation newspaper. His hard-hitting and irreverent column, 'A Sunny Day' has acquired a wide following. He also writes for *Business Daily* and a number of other publications, on issues relating to the economy, management, governance and society.

Sunny is a member of the Advisory Board of Strathmore Business School, Eastern Africa's first world-class business school. He teaches corporate strategy as an Executive Fellow at the school, and leads a flagship strategy course for chief executives and business leaders.

Sunny is married to Shriti, and they have one son, Vivek.

Congratulations!

By purchasing an original of this book, you are supporting and encouraging African writers. If you suspect it has been copied or pirated, please contact the publishers:

- Visit our website: **www.storymojaafrica.com**
- Or write to:

Storymoja
P.O. Box 264-00606
Sarit Centre, Nairobi, Kenya

Storymoja books are published by No Boundaries Ltd., an ethical, indigenous company formed by a collective of writers committed to promoting African writing of world-class standards.

First published in September 2007 as a Storymoja imprint by No Boundaries Ltd. P. O. Box 264-00606, Sarit Centre, Nairobi, Kenya.

ISBN 9966-7245-1-6

CROWN YOUR CUSTOMER

STORYMOJA BUSINESS

A Storymoja Business Series Book

By SUNNY BINDRA

CONTENT

CHAPTER ONE

Customer Service in Kenya is Appalling

Angela is about to explode. She is at her mechanic's workshop in Nairobi's Industrial Area, staring at her un-repaired car. It is obvious the repair work has not even started. "You promised me Monday. It's Thursday!" she says, struggling not to shout. "I need my car to pick my kids up from school!"

The garage owner's mobile phone keeps ringing. It has a particularly annoying ring-tone that rubs against Angela's frayed nerves like sandpaper. The man seems to be juggling between promises to irate customers. "Why do I come here?" she asks herself as she turns away. She knows the answer: Because every other garage I've tried over the past ten years is exactly the same as this. "*Labda kesho*!" shouts the garage owner cheerfully as she leaves.

A *matatu* comes cruising past, the tout whistling at her as he hangs out of the side. She squeezes in and finds to her dismay that the minivan is already full. The tout starts pushing people aside to make room for her. She sits down gingerly, worried about uninvited physical contact from the men on either side of her. A rap song playing at an insanely high volume sets her teeth on edge.

Her mobile phone beeps. It's a text message from her network provider, asking her to pay her bill to avoid disconnection. She paid last week. She dials the customer care number and is greeted by a cheery message: "All our customer service representatives are busy at the moment. Please wait to be served. Your call is important to us. Please wait. Press '1' to hear about our new product range. Your call is important to us. Please wait." Angela hangs up. The last time she believed them and waited, she was on the line for 13 minutes before a rep "became available".

She becomes aware that the minivan has not moved for some time, and the driver is muttering obscenities. She looks out of her window and sees a line of cars a kilometre long ahead of them. Her frustration grows. She will be very, very late picking up the children from school. Forty-five minutes later the queue has edged along sufficiently to reveal the problem. There is a gaping trench in the main road blocking a whole lane. She remembers seeing some unidentified workers digging it ten days ago. They seem to have left whatever they were doing unfinished, leaving a yawning trench. This is peak traffic hour and the tailback caused by this negligence is huge.

Angela arrives at the school an hour late. All the children have left, apart from her two huddled in a corner fighting back tears. The teacher who has had to stay back to mind them is stone-faced. Mumbling apologies,Angela gathers her children.The teacher hands her a school circular. It says that the school has raised fees by 30 per cent from next term, and that school uniforms and meals, which she has to pay for, are now compulsory.

Back at home she feeds her children. After that is done, she finally puts up her feet to recover from a day fraught with bad experiences.

A little later her husband Bob arrives. He looks frustrated. "I came home early", he says. "There was nothing to do at the office. The printer didn't show up with our marketing brochures. Yet again. They're two weeks late. I don't know how we'll distribute them before the big launch next week. When we call, the *$&*# doesn't answer his phone. That is the last time we do a big print job in Kenya. We've already called someone in Dubai for the next time."

He sees the tiredness on her face. "Let's put the kids to bed early and go out for dinner. We need a treat. Let's try the new Italian place." Angela's spirits lift. A nice, quiet meal is just what they need to recover their spirits.

That evening they walk into the new restaurant that has received rave reviews. It is busy. The maitre d' looks them up and down sniffily and opens the daily booking sheet. He slams it shut and walks off quickly. They realise that they are expected to follow. He leads them to a table in a far corner. Angela tries not to notice that they are next to the toilets. She also tries not to notice that the same sniffy man is now virtually swooning with delight and twanging a fake accent to a large group of *wazungu* who have walked in. They clearly don't have a booking, but she sees him remove a 'reserved' sign from a prime window table for them.

She looks around. The décor is nice, but the place is not yet finished. Their corner has exposed wiring in the ceiling and sloppy paintwork. Not wanting to ruin her evening, she looks away. The menu is ornate and extensive. But much of it is written in Italian and with no English translation offered. She asks a waiter to explain: he has no idea, and goes back to the kitchen to ask.

Her pasta arrives, but Bob's steak does not. He asks her to start eating before it gets cold. Ten minutes later she's nearly done, but he's still waiting and beginning to fume. He stands up and summons the maitre d', who listens to his complaint without uttering a word. The maitre d' turns away and goes to the kitchen. Another ten minutes later, the steak arrives. After his first bite, Bob drops his fork with an angry exclamation. He had asked for his steak to be well done; but inside, it is pink and raw.

Angela starts to complain, but the sniffy manager frowns at them from across the room like they are insects who cannot possibly appreciate the finer things in life.

"That's it", shouts Bob. "We're leaving." He throws some money on the table. The waiters watch them go in sullen silence. Not one word of explanation or apology is offered.

***

Angela and Bob are you. If you are a middle-class consumer in Kenya, their day was your typical day. If you are a rich Kenyan, your life as a customer might be a little better: the establishments you frequent are a little more polished at handling their customers (but not much). If you are a poor Kenyan, your experiences can be immeasurably worse. If you don't have much money, you are not supposed to expect anything approaching good service. In middle or high class establishments, poor people daring to expose their vernacular accents or unfashionable clothes or who extract their hard earned money from their bosoms, are treated as though they entered the place by accident. Angela's and Bob's day, just described, would seem like a joyride to the average poor Kenyan, who is ignored if he stays quiet and abused if he speaks up.

Horror stories from the public services are not news. We all have our own. We have all gone to public offices trying to complete a trivial but necessary task, and found ourselves shunted from counter to counter and office to office. We have been to the post office where the clerk takes the document you are offering, stamps it with a loud bang, and throws it onto a large pile without once looking at you. We have waited for weeks, even months, for a telephone land-line to be repaired. We have screamed with genuine terror when our ID card was stolen - knowing the travails that await us in getting a new one.

We lurch from one example of customer *disservice* to another - every day. And this does not just happen in the public sector. As Angela's and Bob's day showed, our supposedly customer-focused, supposedly profit-maximising private businesses are often the worst offenders.

We've all waited for a building contractor to show up and start work as promised. Showed up on time at a doctor's surgery for a 10.40am appointment (why are they so precise?), only to be finally seen at 12.23pm. Wondered why at even top international banks only three of the eight available counters are working when the line of waiting customers is about a mile long. Visited fancy shops manned by no fewer than six assistants - all of whom look bored to tears, yet none of whom are bored enough to serve you. This in full view of the proprietor, who looks more bored than everyone. And I'm not sure anyone in Kenya has found a garage that is prompt, friendly and *honest*.

The customer, we are told as children, is king. Anyone who has spent some of his or her life in Kenya could be forgiven for screaming at that fanciful notion. Here, the customer is a serf, a pauper, a desperado.

Customer service, it appears, is a catastrophe in these parts. People just don't seem to "get it" that the much neglected, much abused and taken-for-granted person walking into your business could walk out forever. Leaving you to blame the government, political turmoil and high power prices for the collapse of your business.

If there is a behaviour that captures the lamentable state of customer service, it is this: the universal refusal to make eye contact. When you have no intention of serving customers well, your eyes tell the story. In Kenya, people make a career of avoiding looking at you.

It is amazing that this state of affairs continues. It is so stupid that it almost can't be happening. We claim to be a nation of businesspeople, but do we understand the basic essence of business? How can anyone who wants to make sustained profits neglect and mistreat customers like this?

How bad is the problem? And are there organisations that "get" customer service, and have happy customers? Of course there are - but not many. In preparation for this book, I have been asking a question of many people I meet: "Please write down five examples of great customer service you have experienced in Kenya."

I have to report that not one of the dozens of people I asked got past two examples; most stopped at just one. Some had none.

CHAPTER TWO

The Customer is the Monarch of the Marketplace

A business leader once made the most disarmingly simple definition of business that I am aware of. *Shareholders look after employees. Employees look after customers. Customers look after shareholders.* That's it. Business defined in a very small nutshell. But you'll need to read it again and think deeply about that simple advice.

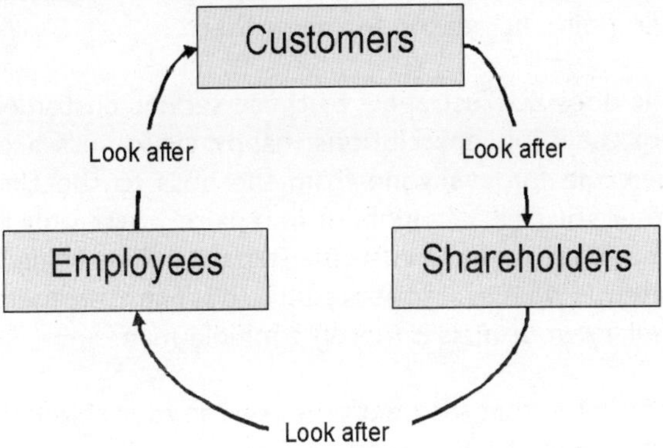

The diagram above depicts it visually. For the small business, it's very straightforward. The shareholder and the top employee are usually the same person. If you are such an owner-manager, you must fixate yourself and your staff on the customer, and nothing else.

If you are a shareholder in a larger company, note who's looking after you. Not your board of directors pontificating in palatial boardrooms. Not the CEO sitting in a top-level strategy workshop deep in the Mara. No, your dividend comes from one person and one person alone: the CUSTOMER.

If you're an employee, note what your mission in life is: to look after customers. To grab them, thrill them and keep them. For life. Yes, I know: you're also supposed to fight competitors, manage suppliers, make plans, delegate, attend meetings, write reports and generally buzz around being busy all day long. But do you have a reason for living? Yes: her name is CUSTOMER. This person enriches the shareholder who pays your salary. You can engage in all the time-passing activity you like: if you aren't looking after customers, you have no point, no reason for being there.

This does not just apply to those serving customers as part of their job descriptions: happy customers are job number one for everyone from the boss to the cleaner. Whether you're in accounts or in repairs, you're only there because you're part of a customer-satisfaction machine. That, ultimately, is what everyone is paid to do. The customer pays your salary; your boss is merely a middle-man.

Remember that the next time you eat your chips while a customer waits to be served.

Finally, if you're a customer, observe that you are the nexus, the critical link, in the virtuous circle. You look after if you are looked after. You pay the business-owner his return; you must in turn be given value by that person's company. So why should you be the most docile part of the chain? Why do you acquiesce in your own enforced misery?

Simple stuff. Yet so difficult to achieve. But people do achieve it, sometimes painfully, sometimes slowly. Those who try *do* get there.

This applies to businesses of all sizes and shapes. From the one-man artisan to the sprawling regional multinational employing thousands, your primary purpose in life is the same: to keep customers happy. That's why you show up at your place of work every day.

If you think there is something else that's more important in business life, you should pack up now.

This is not an isolated view. According to economists, customers are the monarchs of the marketplace. In a market economy it is not big companies or governments that call the shots. Customer tastes, expressed as shilling votes, direct the use of resources. Companies' profits and losses are the rewards and penalties of the marketplace. Customers are firmly in the driving seat.

In Kenya, of course, you would be forgiven for shouting a loud "Say what?" at this point. Here, things appear to be a little different. Kicked here and there by big business and big government, customers could be forgiven for feeling more like vagabonds than rulers.

To get good treatment from a bank, you usually have to be a high-net-worth customer; otherwise you are looked upon as part of the rabble that crowds the banking halls and stains the floors, creating a nuisance. Lawyers are known to pay scant attention to most clients' cases, and have earned a reputation for running off with their money. Many manufacturers produce goods of a quality that has stayed at the same lamentable standard for decades – and then grab microphones and headlines to invoke patriotic fervour when better quality imports threaten them. How do we explain this anomaly? Why is bad customer care allowed to survive for so long in Kenya?

The same economists would have a ready answer for us. Businesspeople are few, and customers are many. Economic power is based upon *scarcity*: what is scarce, commands power. In most sectors in Kenya, there is simply not enough competition to provide customers with real choices. We have made considerable progress in this regard in recent years, but not enough. Monopolistic practices still dog many industries. Competition is still muted rather than intense; producers still get into cosy arrangements. In these circumstances, taking customers for granted is no surprise. You don't lose a customer when he or she has nowhere else to go.

Until recently, if you wanted your milk and newspaper early in the morning, you usually had to rely on the local kiosk. There would only be one such kiosk in your immediate area, so you had no real choice in the matter. The kiosk man, having a captive customer base, could be unreliable and unruly - it didn't matter. You'd still have to use him.

Life is a little different these days. Companies are falling over themselves to deliver things to your house. The newspaper publishers themselves run home-delivery services at no extra charge. You can order things off the internet. Retail outlets have proliferated; even petrol stations stock a wide range of convenience products in their forecourt shops. Customers have more choice and they exercise it.

So are the local kiosk-owners out of business? Certainly, the rude and undependable ones will have made a welcome exit. But the ones that have a special bond with their local customers - based on warm and reliable service, or friendly opening hours - still prosper.

In this respect, competition is a market cleanser and we should all applaud when new competitors appear - at all levels of business. Newly-arrived Virgin Atlantic Airways will make life uncomfortable for all the incumbent airlines, and more comfortable for customers. The established airlines have been forced to respond. You can bet your last shilling that they are all frantically examining what makes them competitive (or not): their profit margins; their cost structures; their service delivery; their operational effectiveness; their relationship with their customers.

This is precisely the point of competition and the reason we should embrace it. Competition introduces the fear of imminent demise to even the steadiest, most long-standing players. It forces them to rethink, to re-examine, and to reinvent. It forces wastage, unnecessary cost and abnormal profits out of the system. It creates new interest in customers and their needs. And those customers start smiling again, sometimes after years of abuse.

In industry after industry, we see the sweeping benefits of competition. In banking, there has been a revolution in charges, opening hours, delivery channels and tailored loan products. Remarkably, much of this activity caters to those customers who were once abandoned in droves - the poor. From a variety of banks, they are now receiving respect along with products tailor-made to address their needs.

Equally, banks at the other end of the spectrum - those focusing on high-net-worth individuals and corporate customers - are designing new banking channels and relationship programmes that are taking much of the stress out of banking. The customer is basking in all the sudden attention.

In telephony, there has been an explosion of voice and data offerings at previously unheard-of prices. Did we ever imagine that we could bank on a Saturday afternoon, or by SMS? Or that we could call America for a few shillings per minute? In yesteryear, the old monopolists who had those industries in their paws would have told you none of those things were even possible.

The best thing that happened to East African Breweries was the arrival of South African Breweries. The pitch battle that took place then was the making of our own brewer: it reinvented its processes and reconnected with its customers, and came out of the war a hard and lean player ready to take on all comers.

So competition is great for the customer. But that does not explain why we have such dreadful service in industries that are seemingly very competitive: restaurants; car-repair garages; building contractors; and many others. Given the range of choices out there, why are they mostly so bad?

That points us to another culprit. If you are a customer complaining about bad service, you need look no further than the mirror to find out who's *really* to blame.

The truth is, here in Kenya we have some of the most meek, timid and uncomplaining customers in the world. No matter what intimidations and humiliations we suffer from businesspeople, we neither complain nor withdraw our business. No matter what run-arounds we are given and what lies we are told, we don't speak out. Some customers do, but there aren't enough of them. The vast majority just take it on the chin and come back for another punch the following day.

Why we are like that, I have no idea. It would take a bigger book than this one to explain the strange phenomenon of the Acquiescent Kenyan Customer. The same thesis would, I am sure, explain why we Kenyans keep voting for leaders who denude us and retard our progress. After every election, we see the inadequacies of those we elect; yet we queue up to vote for the same people again. In the same depressingly predictable way, citizen-consumers keep giving their shilling votes to awful businesses.

Equally, we (the ones complaining) are all employees or business owners somewhere ourselves. What standards do we set ourselves in those roles? Do we strive to provide immaculate service to our customers? Or are we just as slipshod and careless as everyone else? If so, we have no right to complain when we are on the receiving end of poor customer care.

The bottom line is that poor customer service is no-one's fault but our own. The real fault lies not in our stars, our state or our structures. The real fault lies in our standards. Customer service is just one of many interactions in a society. If we are unable to treat each other with respect and courtesy in our politics, on our roads, in our family lives - why should we expect to do so in business?

Business, however, has a natural advantage: there is an in-built incentive to treat people well, because all parties benefit. It is that incentive we should use to spark a revolution in human interaction in Kenya.

CHAPTER THREE

The Huge Business Opportunity Poor Customer Service Offers

What you've read so far may be sending you into a state of deep gloom. Yet if you own a business of any size, or work for one, there is every reason to rejoice.

How so?

Recall what was asserted in Chapter Two: business power comes from scarcity. The more unique or distinctive your offering, the more power you have over customers. On the other hand, the more ubiquitous or common-place your business model, the less likely you are to make any real money out of it. Sustained success comes from what in management-speak is called a *distinctive value proposition*: an offering that gives customers a unique pay-off.

But here's the issue: distinctive value propositions are not easy to find (if they were, everyone would be offering them). Scarcity is itself scarce, in other words. The old days of firms having monopoly power without any effort on their parts - sole-operator licenses, for example, or individual control of a scarce resource - are disappearing. These days, uniqueness must be designed and worked for.

Modern businesses try to create a less obvious and more subtle kind of scarcity. Some work hard on their *reputation* by building a distinctive *brand.* It is very difficult for any competitor to match the Coca-Cola brand, for instance: there is more than a century of brand-building and marketing spend behind it (that's why Coke only has one equally large and equally long-lived competitor - others can't meet that sort of entry requirement).

Other firms work on their uniqueness by developing distinctive *skills and capabilities* over time. These firms differentiate themselves from the chasing pack by working out better, more effective ways of doing things: unique business processes; unusually well-deployed systems; or the business knowledge contained in the heads of key employees. In fact, being better at attracting, motivating and retaining the best people is a capability that is often the most difficult to match.

The point is: companies work very hard to be distinctive, and often search high and low for features with which to differentiate their products and services. It is through differentiation that superior profit streams become available, not by having a one-of-many blandness.

And that's why, whatever your industry, your business is sitting on a goldmine in Kenya. You don't have to look further than your nose in order to find a way of being unique. SUPERB CUSTOMER SERVICE is the feature that the country is crying out for. If you can provide it, you will win over an army of customers. If you can provide it, your products will in all probability be able to command a price premium. If you can provide it, you will have found the keys to the kingdom: the kingdom in which the customer reigns supreme, and in which you, the business owner, are in full charge of the treasury coffers.

In competitive situations, the firm that can develop the strongest emotional bond with customers tends to be the one that races ahead of the others. And in Kenya, customers like Angela and Bob (and you and me) tend to feel pretty emotional.

Amidst the sea of docility, an anger is growing. It's an anger that says: "I've had enough! I won't take any more of this crap. Either you serve me properly, courteously and efficiently, or I stop buying."

This is precisely the emotion that could make you a fortune. Here is what you need to do: make your business the very best one in your industry at caring for customers. Make yours the one that exudes the greatest warmth and friendliness. Make yours the one that customers cross town to visit simply because it's so nice dealing with you. Make yours the one that they joyfully recommend to their friends. *Make yours the one that consistently offers the best, most unique customer service in town.*

Wait a minute, you ask: does this stuff work? Sounds too easy to be true. The answer is more complicated: it *does* work; but it *isn't* easy.

To understand this, consider first an example from far away. There is a company called Southwest Airlines in the USA. It set up shop in 1972, and was the first airline to 're-imagine' the airline business. Its revolutionary goal was to give the freedom of flying to ordinary Americans; its breakthrough was to dramatically reduce the cost of flying. If you wanted to fly with Southwest, you didn't call anyone to book a ticket: you merely showed up at the airport. Southwest has such frequent flights that you simply hop onto the next one. With your remarkably cheap ticket in hand, you would begin to notice Southwest's no-frills model. There would be no fancy lounge to wait in; no pre-assigned seating; no 'free' meals on board.

If Southwest had been a Kenyan airline, we would have called it the '*matatu* in the sky'. We would have expected that the low price would lead to commensurately awful customer service. And we would probably have been right. But Southwest didn't do it that way. It may have cut out (largely unnecessary) features in order to keep the price low, but it made *no compromise on friendly service*, none whatsoever. Quite the opposite: Southwest set out to offer the best service of any airline in America.

This is Southwest's basic statement of purpose: it is "dedicated to the highest standard of customer service delivered with a sense of warmth, friendliness, individual pride and company spirit". Notice what's missing: no mention of the shareholders and stakeholders that every company feels beholden to. Southwest is beholden to the customer, first and foremost. Southwest offers smiles and genuine concern. It knows that the shareholder will be looked after by the happy customer. Does it work? Well, Southwest is consistently the world's most profitable airline. It is now the leading domestic US carrier. Since 1987, it has had the fewest overall customer complaints. It became America's 3rd most admired corporation in 2006. Not too shabby.

What about the shareholders - are they content? Overjoyed! Southwest was 'Money' magazine's best-performing stock for the past thirty years. If my father had invested USD 10,000 for me in Southwest Airlines in 1972, it would have been worth USD 10,200,000 in 2002. Needless to say, he didn't - that's why I'm writing this book.

What about here in Kenya - does emphasising customer service work? Well, a precious few do make outstanding customer service their key competitive advantage in Kenya, and we have a notable home-grown example to look at. The Serena Hotels Group focuses obsessively on training its staff to give pleasure, consistently and unrelentingly, to its clients. Good customer care seems to have entered the bloodstream of most Serena employees. The chain has a legion of repeat visitors who will stay nowhere else. It is now the most successful hotel chain by some distance in this part of the world, and has just opened the region's outstanding hotel property in Kampala.

This is no coincidence: you need only look at the joy simultaneously present on the faces of shareholders, staff and customers to see the power of the virtuous circle (introduced in Chapter Two) in action. Shareholders have ensured that employees are focused first and foremost on keeping hotel clients pleased; those customers are in turn toasting the shareholders by keeping hotel beds and lobbies full.

Is good service only the exclusive remit of large, successful and well-funded organisations like Southwest and Serena, who can afford to provide it? Not at all. They are large, successful and well-funded *because* they are focused so obsessively on their customers! So no matter what the size of your business, the keys to the kingdom are in your hand.

Great customer service can be found in the most modest of places. At the other end of the scale, there was a kiosk called Gatundu's. You may not have heard of it, but it was the favoured lunchtime home of generations of school children in Parklands.

Why? Because it served excellent chips and *bhajias*, hygienically, quickly and efficiently, day in, day out. The proprietors knew their target market, and they served it with great enthusiasm. (Sadly, Gatundu's was the victim of the government's zeal in eradicating great little businesses: it was flattened by council *askaris*.)

Kenyans who buy modest plots on which to build modest homes also enjoy good customer service - in an unlikely place. Nairobi's Gikomba market is where city-dwellers go to search for cheap building supplies. As you park your car, enthusiastic young men will bring samples of timber, sheets of glass, paint - whatever you are looking for. And after you've placed your order and are waiting for things to be gathered or cut to size, you will be offered a cup of tea, and can even have your car polished while you wait!

Another public market, Kariokor, offers different little delights. Meat lovers will tell you that you can get full just sampling free morsels of *nyama choma*. Competition is intense in the market, so each meat seller tries to earmark his 'regulars' and offer them something distinctive: speedy service if they're in a hurry or a cup of porridge to supplement the meat if they're on a limited budget.

In the boardrooms of great corporations, and in the daily bustle of popular markets, some people have cottoned on to some essential facts about business: you can't go wrong if you are always worrying about your customers; you can't go broke delighting your buyers. Give them attention, give them understanding, and give them unexpected little joys. In turn, they will give you success. Whether you run a café or a conglomerate, whether you are a local peddler or a regional powerhouse, great customer service is within your reach.

Sounds simple - but is it easy to do? There's the catch. Outstanding customer service is by no means easy to pull off. If it was, everyone would already be doing it. There's a mountain to climb, but the peak can be reached using a step-by-step approach. To find out how, read on.

CHAPTER FOUR

Ten Key Lessons in Superb Customer Service

Is there a 'formula' that delivers great customer service? Not at all. There is no silver bullet, no magic potion, no methodology or training that guarantees you can be outstanding in this critical discipline.

Great customer care is a philosophy, a way of thinking and being, a deep-seated conviction. Your heart must light up when observing a happy customer; equally, your intestines must twist into a knot when you see your organisation tormenting a customer. That cannot be taught; it can only be felt.

We need to understand the genesis of the problem. There is no shortage of people who can tell you what to do: there is a large body of knowledge and an array of techniques and best practice that you can deploy to develop good customer service in your organisation. There is also no shortage of training courses and seminars available on the subject – they happen every week, and leading organisations spend millions on them. But this is not a problem you can buy your way out of.

You cannot buy the conviction that customer service is the critical factor that will drive the long-term success of your business. And without conviction, there is little motivation to change or to put customer service at the top of your company's agenda. But if you are convinced, here are a few sensible things for you to consider that can put you on the right path. They are commonsensical, even banal, yet could unlock great success for you and your organisation. They are summarised here as 10 essential lessons in building great customer service.

Lesson 1: Start at the top

Show me an organisation that is arrogant, aloof and out of touch with its customers, and I will show you a boss who is arrogant, aloof and out of touch with his customers. It is all about leadership. We recruit our business leaders on the strength of their academic credentials and the big-name companies on their CVs. We assess their ability to crunch numbers and manage projects. We almost never check whether they are any good at handling customers. That is a skill too "soft" to bear examination.

An organisation is a reflection of its leadership. We learn by example, and tailor our behaviour to match that of those holding power. So if the top team devotes its time to financial analysis, planning acquisitions and managing major capital expenditures – don't be too surprised to find customer-facing staff painting their nails and surfing websites. If the CEO finds dealing with pesky customers an irritation, so will his frontline people. It's a manifestation of the same problem – the inability to understand the absolute centrality of the customer in any business equation.

This holds true whether you run a shop or a multinational. If you yourself are bad at dealing with customers, so will your staff. The little monkeys do as the big monkey does. If you put customer interactions at the bottom of your daily tasks list; if you find handling complaints a distraction; if you often lose your temper with customers who complain too much: well, that's exactly the kind of organisation you will create around you, whether you want to or not.

This is a fact: the leaders of great businesses spend a great deal of time meeting, charming, and understanding their customers. There isn't anything they regard as more fundamental to the business.

Why is it that in so many companies the parking spaces closest to the front door, and with nice roof shades, are reserved for senior executives and directors, while a barking *askari* will send customers to the farthest reaches of the parking lot where their cars will bake in the tropical sun? What does this tell us about who is the Most Important Person in that company?

So, if the business you own is terrible at customer care, you won't have to look too far to find the real reason. The problem is almost certainly YOU.

Lesson 2: Make customer service everyone's job

Customer service is NOT what the Customer Service Department does. Yet in most large organisations that is all it is. Customers complaining? Pass 'em on to Customer Service. Set up a special phone number for the whining ingrates to call. Put up a desk. Appoint a manager. Send the reps on a course.

This is a particularly brainless way of attacking the issue, yet it is the one most organisations follow. And when it doesn't work, the Customer Service Manager is sacked and the department overhauled. That particular position must have one of the highest turnover rates in management.

Why doesn't it work? Because you can't segregate the management of customers. You can't fence it off and put it into a nice neat corner where the people look pretty, wear smart uniforms and have pleasant accents. Good customer service is 'global' or it is nothing. It is done by everyone or it is pointless. And it is spearheaded, crucially, by the person at the very top.

Yes, you can have 'customer-facing' people who deal with customers on a daily basis and have the knowledge and training to handle them. There's nothing wrong with that. What is painful is when they are the ONLY people a customer can meet. What that leads to is the decision-makers in the business gradually getting cut off from the customer, and making big decisions based on very faulty information. This matters less in a small business where the owner-manager is always in close proximity to everyday transactions with customers. In a large, multi-layered business, however, a growing distance between management and customer can be fatal.

Lesson 3: Make customer abuse a serious offence

Is it OK to forgive the occasional lapse in dealing with customers? In Kenya, it seems very forgivable indeed, judging by the number of people around who annoy customers to distraction, but still keep their jobs. But if you're serious about customer service, you must treat transgressions in this area as seriously as you would fraud or abuse of office. If you caught an employee with his hands in the till, or with his hands on another employee, I imagine that employee's future with your company to be limited in the extreme.

It should be exactly the same for a member of staff who ignores, neglects, argues with, or insults a customer. Anything of that nature should be an instant show-stopper which leads to an immediate meeting with the boss. This is the only way to instil the discipline of handling customers correctly. Otherwise, it's all talk and no trousers.

Lesson 4: Teach and keep teaching the basics

Please don't assume that customer service is something that needs an occasional lecture from the boss. You do have to teach and re-teach the essential elements. Your people must understand and have:

- The right manner and body language
- Deep knowledge about your company and its products
- Scripts that help them address specific complaints and predictable problems
- A clear sense of the escalation procedure - how and when to move the problem upward in the organisation

Who should teach this? Ideally, you should need no outside help in learning and teaching good customer service. It should be intrinsic, a conviction, a way of doing things that is a fundamental value observed by all. Yet there is some merit in considering outside intervention. We do have a wide range of teaching and training organisations. Some of them, let it be said, you should not touch even with a very long pole. Others have designed thoughtful programmes that might well make a difference to your people.

But please do not enrol your employees, at great cost, on a training programme that teaches customer service in a dry, theoretical and methodological way. Those programmes carry little value. The training should come at two levels:

1. Philosophy - teach why customer care isn't just the most important thing in the business: it IS the business.
2. Execution - teach how to do it well, every day and in every way.

If you can find a training provider that has creative and interesting ways of teaching these things to your staff, in 'live' or at least realistic settings, and using well-designed role-play situations, you may have a chance of making the investment pay off.

If you run a small organisation without a large training budget, then you must do it the old-fashioned way: by yourself, painstakingly and obsessively. You must motivate your staff to do it better, reward successes, punish and correct mistakes. You must act as the *parent* teaching good behaviour. The techniques are the same, and have been known to parents since the dawn of time.

Lesson 5: Pick out the naturals

There are some people on this planet who are unnaturally gifted. Offering great service is in their very nature. They are joyful when those they serve are joyful; they grieve deeply when their customers feel let down. They need almost no customer-care training; they were born with it. You will know them when you see them: they are full of smiles, and are gentle and good natured.

Such people are the lifetime-award-winners of customer service. If you weighed them in gold and paid them that amount, you would still be ahead. These are the ones you need to build your customer care delivery around: they can spearhead and lead your efforts.

Don't worry if they are lacking in other areas, or have weak CVs. Other skills can be taught; this one you can only excel in by being born with it. So when you see a 'smiler', hire her: you'll worry about what to do with her later.

I know a man who tells me that he only persists with his bank (a leading multinational) because of the presence of one such lady. She makes it all worthwhile; her smiles are so bright and her manner so warm that she overwhelms the monstrosity behind her. It's worth it because of the person, not the institution. Here's the rub, though: should she leave that bank, so will this customer.

Even if you find it difficult to find many naturals of this sort, do make sure the first person your customer sees is a 'smiler'. It makes a world of difference. One of the city's better-known restaurants employs an extremely dour and perpetually gloomy-faced lady to receive patrons at the door; a fundamental error that sets the tone for the diner's experience.

That tells us a great deal about the psychology of customer service. Great-natured people make up for bad institutions; bad-natured people ruin great institutions. You might be very brainy or charismatic, well aware of the critical importance of customer service - but that doesn't mean you can handle customers well. For some people, however, being nice, warm, attentive and concerned is not a feat, it comes naturally. When you see those people, grab them with both hands, employ them and make sure you keep them.

Lesson 6: Cut out the insincerity

There is a disease around that's so deep-rooted I wonder if we'll ever cure ourselves of it. This malady is called *management-speak*. It causes the sufferer to confuse words with action, and replace vigour with verbiage. So you will hear the victim talk incessantly about *customer-centric excellence* and *enterprise-wide customer-delight programmes* and other gibberish of this nature. All of this fancy-sounding material will be posted on websites, written into mission statements, placed in corporate receptions.

Warning: In my experience, the businesses that are MOST fond of management-speak are the WORST at actually looking after customers.

Great customer care is not about flowery talk and mindless jargon: it's about FEELING and ACTION. It's a way of thinking, and a way of being. At its best, it's an entirely natural process. Of course, large and complex enterprises find it difficult to ensure a consistent level of customer service, across management layers, divisions and geographies. So they do need to have complicated programmes that inculcate and deliver good service. But here's the point: what you're trying to replicate is something quite simple and natural. It's about being good to people. Is that really so hard to do? Just because your company is large, it doesn't mean you have to live on another planet. It's still about basic human interaction - a skill many corporate androids seem to lose as time goes on and their companies get larger.

Language matters. Words have impact, and should not be ignored. Be clear, simple and sincere in your statements.

Don't hide behind falsehoods and weasel-words - just say and write what you mean. Customers understand plain-speaking people, and like it when you keep it simple.

Here is how one company says it:

"Focus on the user and all else will follow. From its inception, Google has focused on providing the best user experience possible. While many companies claim to put their customers first, few are able to resist the temptation to make small sacrifices to increase shareholder value. Google has steadfastly refused to make any change that does not offer a benefit (to users)."

Last time I checked (2006), Google was clocking USD 3 billion in profits.

Lesson 7: Understand the context

Good customer care has certain universal requirements: warmth, friendliness, genuine concern and sincerity are ALWAYS necessary in pretty much all circumstances. But there are many other service attributes that you will need to address. Which of these you give most emphasis depends on your business context. Different businesses throw up different opportunities for good customer care; it's up to you to study your customers deeply and understand what they *really* want.

- If you run a garage, HONESTY is the most important attribute every customer is looking for. Let's face it, your line of work is not renowned for sincerity - quite the opposite. We are used to lies about when the car will be ready, lies about how much it will cost, even lies about what is really wrong. A garage that actually means what it says and adheres to an honesty policy will really stand out in the eyes of customers.

• If you are a contractor, repair service or installer, your industry's reputation for lack of candour is even worse. Why do you never show up WHEN YOU SAID YOU WOULD? In this industry, the normal practice is to take on more work than you can handle, and promise everyone you'll "start on Monday". To all customers except (perhaps) one, you are lying through your teeth. Lying isn't a basis for a meaningful relationship with a customer. I have no idea why contractors do this. Why is gathering widespread hatred so acceptable to you?

• If you run a bank or a utility company, it's about SPEED. Let's face it, people don't really enjoy being in your establishment. They come there because it's necessary. They want to finish their business and leave to get on with their real work. So your customer-care Task No. 1 is to allow them to do so. For this, you need streamlined, efficient processes. You want to minimise queues. If there's one thing that's guaranteed to stick in the throat of every customer in a bank, it's why there are so few tellers available when queues are so long (this applies equally to supermarkets). Conventional management thinking worries about the labour cost of manning all the teller points at all times of day. But why does it not worry about the lost goodwill? If someone actually sat down to calculate the cost of annoying your core customers on a regular basis, that equation would look very different. Alternatively, if queues really are a part of life, at least make the experience of being in your institution less tedious and, dare we say it, even enjoyable! Kenyan banks now often provide television screens in banking halls - unfortunately they tend to play dreary corporate videos and puff pieces that only increase the viewer-queuer's desire to end his life there and then.

• If you run a restaurant or eatery of some sort, the most neglected service attribute is ATTENTIVENESS. You've all experienced it: you try to get a waiter's attention because you need something. You might as well wait for the return of the messiah - that might happen a whole lot sooner. Why? Because Kenyan waiters all acquire tunnel vision as soon as they start their jobs: they look straight ahead, and nowhere else. Or huddle in large groups in the corner, giggling and whispering. You could even climb onto your table, take off all your clothes and dance *Lingala*: they probably still won't see you. If you own the restaurant, this is crazy. The most basic thing you need to teach waiters in this business is lateral vision - how to keep looking around to see who needs you. If you can't do that, please take your team to plough a field instead. At least it's a business where you need to look straight ahead to get it right.

• If you are a low-cost provider serving a mass market, the biggest thing you can focus on is RESPECT. The poor are always the most ignored and the most abused segment of society. They are often disenfranchised, just because they lack individual buying power. But intelligent businesses have understood the power the poor hold as a mass, and have created products and packaging that suit the low-income buyer. The tendency, nevertheless, is to somehow treat low-value customers as less than human, as though they lack the feelings or discernment of the higher-spending classes. This is nonsense. You can make a lot of money supplying the poor; you can make even more supplying it with respect and esteem. Kenya's Equity Bank has sparked a banking revolution by understanding this simple fact.

• If you run a hospital, you are dealing first and foremost with FEAR. People don't come to your place to have a good time; they come in a state of agitation and apprehension. Your top task is to reassure, to soothe, to calm. Gertrude's Children's Hospital takes this very seriously, knowing that where children are involved, fear takes on a new dimension. A businessman told of the time his son had convulsions and was rushed to Gertrude's. Although he had never been there before, his son was immediately taken into intensive care, no questions asked. It was only after his son was out of danger that the man was very politely and unobtrusively asked to start the registration process and arrange payment. The hospital put his child's life first. He remembers, and he tells everyone.

Good service is not terribly useful in isolation. You do have to provide decent product quality, an accessible location, and a fair price amongst other attributes. But great service is a special attribute. It can make up for weakness in other areas; and it is often the difference between the merely good and the truly great business.

So, whatever your line of business and whatever your market segment, understanding the elements of service to put most emphasis on is actually very straightforward: just PAY GREAT ATTENTION to your customers. Think deeply about what they need, what they love, what they detest. Walk in their shoes for a while. Understand their lives, their aspirations, their fears. And then do the needful.

Lesson 8: It's OK to get it wrong; but not to *keep* getting it wrong

Even the best business person can't sit down and plan for immaculate customer service. It just isn't possible to foresee every little thing that will constitute great service. Some things will only emerge through experience, in the daily hurly-burly of business. Could you tell that your new billing system would get some details wrong? Only when you started billing. Could you imagine that a particular phrase in your brochure would offend some people? Only when it was in their hands.

There's nothing wrong with not having perfect foresight. There is EVERYTHING wrong with not benefiting from experience. We have all forgiven businesses their minor trespasses; what gets us REALLY mad is when they keep repeating them. Shafting the customer in the same place every week is a real insult; it says: *"I know this annoys you, but I can't be bothered doing anything about it. That's how little I value you."*

A customer of one of the country's largest and oldest banks found that one little thing was the final straw for her. Being a typically tolerant Kenyan, she had put up with poor service for years. But one day she went in to arrange a banker's draft and half-way through the process, noticed that she had misspelled the name of the recipient. The bank's staff snapped at her for wasting their time.

She walked out forever. If you think insulting customers in this way is par for the course, then perhaps only bankruptcy courts can help you.

Lesson 9: Every complaint is a golden opportunity

This is a much-repeated one, but it's only repeated because it's true. We have a natural tendency to take cover when a customer starts complaining. No one likes to be ticked off by some self-righteous oaf. So we hide and hope someone else takes the flak. That may feel natural, but it's extremely short-sighted. A complaint is not a problem; it's a customer coming to you, sitting on a silver platter, with a sign around his neck saying: "Take me - I could be yours for life."

A complaint is a double opportunity: one, a chance to learn what your customers *really* want from your business (which is something you may never learn from your employees, or from other dissatisfied customers who walk out without a word); two, an opportunity to make this particular customer so happy that she will never go anywhere else. In other words, the *complaining customer* is actually that much-sought creature, the *lifetime customer* - in disguise!

How do you remove the disguise? By sitting down calmly with the irate customer and showing great concern. By apologising sincerely for whatever went wrong. By assuring the customer it won't happen again. And then damned well making sure that it DOESN'T happen again. Throw in a cup of tea and plenty of smiles, and you could probably put a lifetime contract on the table and get it signed before the customer leaves.

Lesson 10: Little things matter

Please don't imagine that great service is for those businesses that can afford it. You don't need massive investments in training and Customer Relationship Management systems to be good to customers. Little touches can make all the difference.

I was told of the hardware shop whose manager unfailingly invites any unhappy customer into his private office and apologises profusely, sweetening the customer with candy and biscuits as they chat. His staff members confirm that it never fails. This is a man who understands customer psychology.

I also learnt of the beauty salon in Nairobi that makes sure every customer is greeted by a very friendly (and handsome!) young man, swept into a waiting room, and offered a red rose and a complimentary glass of wine as she waits for her turn. Would you be surprised to learn that the place is always full?

And a customer told me the reason she loves her local supermarket is that attendants there make a real effort to remember customers' names, and greet them very warmly when they see them again. So simple - but it makes a difference.

Customers always appreciate small but meaningful gestures. They *expect* the big things; they *love* the little things. Little things touch their hearts and make them feel special. It won't take you long to think up your own set of little touches. The effort is always worth it.

CHAPTER FIVE

Customer, Crown Thyself

Thus far we have focused on what businesspeople need do to take better care of their customers. That makes sense, because great customer service would help them improve their businesses. But isn't there another stakeholder involved here - the *customer*? The very person who sustains business? What can the customer do to empower himself?

Here's a thought: forget about politicians for a moment - why can't the much-abused customers of Kenya take power?

Kenyan customers, like Kenyan voters, have always been taken for granted. They are meek, gullible, ignorant and easily impressed. This is a dangerous combination. It has caused the paradox of businesses offering appalling service yet raking in obscene profits. They treat you like dirt, but you keep giving them your money. They count on one thing: you aren't going anywhere else.

Customers need to seize back the crown. They hold all the cards. No business, no organisation can survive if its customers do not wish it to. All the votes you need are in your wallet. All you need is to understand how to use those votes and maximise their power.

For one thing, we need more choices on offer. All monopolies must be dismantled, and fresh winds of competition encouraged to blow through the marketplace, to sweep away the dust of inefficiency. Monopolies are a licence to abuse, and we must remove that licence. Customers must understand this and lobby for it. Look at the effects of new competition, in industry after industry: telecommunications, alcoholic beverages, internet services, apparel, and many others. Once, Kenyans had limited choice at high prices; today, at least in some industries, we enjoy a variety of offerings and packages at prices we can afford.

In advanced economies, customers have formed large-scale associations to protect their interests. These associations have millions of members, and do many things for them: they conduct research into the best products on offer and produce buying guides; they lobby government to introduce structural changes in industries; they condemn and boycott producers who turn out products of inferior quality or that harm the environment. They generally make a very constructive nuisance of themselves.

In these countries, even the public sector has been forced to respond. Public institution like railways, power companies and telephone operators have been forced to publish customer charters: clear, binding statements setting out what standards of service the customer has a right to expect. In many cases, these charters have real bite: if a train on the London Underground is more than 15 minutes late (other than through unavoidable circumstances) for example, customers can claim a full refund of the fare paid. If your phone line is not reconnected within a short period, many national telecommunications operators in the United Kingdom now undertake to pay penalties to you. Can you imagine the bracing effect on our state corporations if such charters were enforced here? Overnight they would be forced to modernise their processes and systems, to avoid haemorrhaging money.

To see the effects of customer power, consider the Kenyan horticulture industry. Not so many years ago, Kenyan horticulture was a rag-tag affair of vegetable and flower exporters, churning out produce of highly variable quality and often engaging in questionable activities regarding employees and the environment. Today, the industry is highly organised and focused on product quality, and supplies some of the big names in Europe. Great strides have been made in employee policies and social responsibility. Why? Simply because customers in Europe demanded it. Quality, traceability and policy requirements forced our producers to take a hard look at their processes and practices. They had to comply or lose the business. They complied, and are the stronger for it. The only tragedy is that it took foreign customers to enforce the changes.

Kenyan customers need to climb into that driving seat. They must take their rightful place in the market economy. The time for tolerating shoddiness is past. In Kenya, there are people in business who actually *despise* their customers. There are shopkeepers who look up with distaste any time a customer walks in and shout: "*Nini?*" There are the chief executives who wouldn't be caught dead in the company of some lowly customer unless there are cameras flashing and a photo-opportunity presents itself. Customers, apparently, are beneath them.

Why are these people in business? More importantly, why do YOU allow them to stay in business? Killing a bad business is easy: just stop buying. If most of its customers walk, no business can stay afloat. So why do so many of us lack the basic dignity to boycott businesses that loathe us? Why are we creating the conditions that allow ghastly companies to persist for decades?

What can you do? Just get assertive!

- If a product is consistently poor, stop buying it. Look for alternatives, and encourage your friends to do the same.
- Don't always look for the lowest price; it costs you (and the country) more in the long run if a low price comes coupled with bad service.
- Stop going to a shop if the assistants are surly and the proprietor is unavailable. Walk a little farther, and find a better place.
- If a service provider has let you down, don't just keep quiet: make a racket! Write to the boss, write to the papers, call a radio station.
- If many people in your area are affected by a problem, get together and form an association. Lobby vehemently and persistently. Organise marches and protests (non-violently, of course) outside the offices of the culprits. Embarrass them repeatedly until they do something.
- If you still can't find a business that does things the way you and your fellow customers want them done, start one yourself! If you have any entrepreneurial gumption, opportunity is banging on your door. You have spotted a gap in the market. Get organised, and fill it.

Hit bad businesses where it hurts. But please, please don't accept or acquiesce. The meek are not blessed in the kingdom of the market.

Have you noticed how many CEOs respond personally to customer complaints raised in the national media these days? Or the (very) gradual improvement in customer service standards in some of our better companies? Your complaints give the change more impetus. The best organisations view customer complaints as an opportunity to take leadership. The worst ones see it as a damned nuisance, and need to be consigned to the dustbin of history.

There is a bigger prize at stake. If we learn to fight for our rights as customers, we may learn to fight for them as voters. If, as customers, we begin to see that we can shape economic development, we may begin to understand that as voters, we can transform our political development. We may learn that being nice to people is actually good for the nation.

The point is to recognise the power in our pocket and use it. The ordinary people of this country are the users of services, the beneficiaries of efficient organisation and, more commonly, the victims of failure. Customers of Kenya: take that crown away from politicians and big businesses and put it back on your own heads. Now.

CHAPTER SIX

A New Day for Angela & Bob

Angela is sitting sipping a coffee. She is in the small customer lounge of her mechanic's workshop in Nairobi's Industrial Area. Her car is not quite ready: the team is steam-cleaning the engine and giving the body a complimentary wax polish to make up for the fact that the car repairs are a day late - but at least they had called to warn her. Angela looks at her watch. It'll soon be time to pick her children up from school. But there's still a bit of time to go, so she leans back to read the complimentary newspapers provided by the garage.

The garage owner walks into the lounge with Angela's keys. The car has helpfully been reversed out for her, and is gleaming. There is an invoice discreetly placed on the driver's seat. With a smile Angela writes out a cheque and drives out.

The car has been sprayed with fresh-smelling scent. Angela feels relaxed and ready to take on Nairobi's notorious traffic. Today, she is pleasantly surprised. There are traffic policemen stationed at the worst roundabout on her route, and they are doing a very good job of keeping the traffic moving. She smiles at one as she goes past, and he gives her a cheerful wave.

Her mobile phone rings, and she answers it using her hands-free kit. "Good morning, madam, this is Christine calling from your network provider. I hope I'm not disturbing you. I am a customer service supervisor, and I'm just calling to ask if you are satisfied with the service you are receiving."

Angela responds positively.

"Any areas of improvement you'd like to identify, madam?" persists the supervisor.

"Well, since you're asking, I am receiving my bills a little late in the post...", says Angela.

"I'll look into that personally, madam, and make sure it doesn't keep happening. Did you know that there's a number you can send an SMS message to, and receive your current balance by text immediately? Let me send you the details just now. By the way, we are upgrading the network next week, and you might experience a little disruption on Friday. Please bear with us. It is necessary work that will help us provide a better service."

The call ends, and Angela is pleased she has been forewarned.

Farther down, she notices a commotion on the side of the road. A *matatu* has been stopped on the side of the road by its own passengers! Angela rolls down her window to listen as she waits in the traffic. It seems a tout manhandled a young woman, and the passengers forced the vehicle to stop. They are now busy giving the driver and tout a stern ticking off. Angela smiles: Kenyans have learned to unite and stand up for themselves!

She arrives at the school on time. She sees her two children playing with the class teacher in the compound. The teacher beams at her and hands her a circular. "You're invited to a special parents' meeting to discuss what you feel about the school and raise any questions you might have", says the teacher. "We also want to discuss the issue of fees. Costs have gone up steadily, and we haven't had a fee increase for three years. But we want to discuss what you think about the whole thing. Please do come."

Back at home, she sees that the team that were supposed to realign her TV aerials are already there and working up on the roof. She waves at them cheerily.

A little later her husband Bob arrives. He looks full of beans. "I came home early," he says, "to show you this excellent brochure. Our printing firm has done it again. Look at the quality of this!" He hands her a gleaming full-colour booklet. "Such an excellent company to deal with: the manager brought the packages to me personally, two days earlier than promised! And they have such reasonable prices. We had a nice chat over coffee. Really, they're a credit to the country. We would never use anyone else. Get dressed - I'm taking you out to dinner. Let's try the new Italian place."

That evening they walk into the new restaurant that has received rave reviews. It is busy. The maitre d' walks up to them beaming with delight. "Welcome, welcome - such a pleasure to have you. No booking? No problem, it's still early - plenty of tables available." They are given a prime window table.

She looks around. The décor is stunning, and the place is filling up fast. The menu is ornate and extensive. A waiter helpfully comes to guide them through the menu and make recommendations . Her pasta arrives and looks delectable. Bob's steak, however, is not as well done as he wanted. Three different waiters notice him putting his hand up, and one immediately comes to their table. Bob explains the problem.

"We are so sorry sir," says the waiter. "Give me just five minutes to rectify the problem. In the meantime please have another drink, with our compliments."

Bob sits back, pleased with the response. "Well, I can see we'll be coming back here very often!"

***

That was not a day in heaven: Angela and Bob should be having it right here on Earth, every time the sun comes up. Good, thoughtful service is the basic right of every customer. It is a crying shame that the scenario above is not the common experience of customers. It should be, and can be. All we need to do is refuse to accept that service in Kenya is 'naturally' bad; by accepting that, we are damning ourselves.

What do we learn from Angela & Bob's 'heaven on earth' day, when the service they receive is exemplary everywhere? There are a number of things that are noteworthy:

1. *Even mechanics can be nice to customers.* There is a common perception that occupations like building and repair, or policing, are 'naturally' populated by uncouth roughnecks to whom courtesy is an alien act. Not so: the nature of the work does not matter; the nature of the mind does. We can all be as coarse or as civilised as we choose to be.

2. *Being nice is a nice tactic.* The garage owner, the mobile network, the school and the restaurant in the story have realised something interesting: that if you treat people nicely, you can get away with a lot more! When people feel honoured and respected, they are much more willing to

understand the business-owner's problems. It is really surprising how few companies realise this: that if you consult your customers, they will often agree with you. But if you keep ignoring or annoying them, even a reasonable request will be met with outright hostility.

3. *Think long-term.* For some strange reason, our business owners often can't add up. Most restaurateurs feel serious pain when they have to give out a 'complimentary' to a complaining customer, yet it should be a no-brainer. For the cost of a single drink, the restaurant described here has won the custom of Angela & Bob for life. Not to mention the positive word-of-mouth campaign that they will undoubtedly mount on the restaurant's behalf, free of charge! If you do your calculations properly, you will always invest in customer happiness.

4. *A happy customer is happy to pay.* When we feel we have benefited from a product and service and, critically, consumed it in the right *emotional* setting, we have no problem paying. Most customers resist and delay paying only when they feel short-changed or slighted. Happy customers often don't mind paying more - because great service has altered their perception of value. Suddenly, it's all worth it.

Let's bring the economists in for their final word: if customers keep channelling resources to poor firms, the market will never cleanse itself. We will keep rewarding inefficiency and promoting laxity. Those bad firms will never leave the market, and potentially good ones will never arrive. Therefore, we will retard the development of the economy. The propagation of bad customer care is no minor matter: it has major economic consequences.

***

You will all have your favourites: from coffee houses to vegetable shops, travel agents to hair salons. Think about why you keep going there: invariably, it's the service. Yes, a restaurant has to serve good food; a greengrocer's vegetables must be fresh; a hairdresser must cut your hair the way you want it. But those are 'hygiene' factors; they are 'must-haves'. They are the minimum things a customer expects. They have to be present, but they do not, in themselves, excite customers. That excitement, that warm connection comes from the quality of the human interaction. When people care about you, you care back.

None of these successful businesses finds customer service easy. All of them have to work very hard to sustain what they have. All of them have to plan ahead, design efficient and speedy processes, train and retrain their staff, and inculcate a lasting dedication to pleasing the *mnunuzi.*

They do it well, though, and therefore they succeed. If on the other hand you are part of the colonies of investors and employees who find good customer service just too difficult to pull off: don't worry, history will soon sort out that problem for you. Your customer is waiting to kick you in the butt. At the first opportunity.

Being good to customers is not a one-off event; it's a continuous process of improvement. Kenyan businesses often lapse into complacency. If they win an award, they feel accomplished and relax, thinking they have now 'arrived'. Relaxing your efforts to please customers can be a fatal mistake: your 'departure' can soon follow.

There is no point being good to customers for a limited period. As soon as you are bad to them, they will forget the good days in a flash. But conversely, you can make them forget past failures by ramping up your customer-service levels and convincing them that a new day has dawned.

Many businesses fall into another trap: that of countenancing poor service simply because they are busy. Being busy is often the easiest of excuses: 'we're rushed off our feet.' Customers are expected to be understanding because the queues are long or the orders many. I say: don't be! Good service is your right, no matter how many other people are involved. Your individual transaction with a company may be one of thousands on that day, but it remains sacred nonetheless. An excellent business is excellent in all circumstances - not just when it's easy.

***

When all is said and done, good customer service is not a complicated skill to learn. It's a natural state of being. Being nasty to customers is what is unnatural. The centrality of the customer to all business is a realisation, an understanding. After that, it's a way of life. You would no more upset your customer than you would stamp on your own foot.

Treating customers well is merely a start. It might set the example that helps us to recapture decent behaviour at all levels of our society. It might be the achievement that tips us back into what was once our natural state: a culture that values courtesy, friendliness and mutual concern.

In a country where good service is relatively rare, offering superior customer service is likely to be the one factor that brings in customers who might have gone to your competitors. And because good customer service does not require tons of investment, it is a levelling opportunity – any size or shape of business can deliver excellent service. It is the secret that can transform your business - and it's right under your nose.

So crown your customer, and do it with ceremony and sincerity. And the bottom line? The customer will crown you in turn.

Feedback Feeds Us

Storymoja invites you to comment on this book. We yearn to publish the type of books you'd like to read. Please share your insights and ideas with us.

- Visit our website: ***www.storymojaafrica.com***
- Or write to:

  Storymoja
  P. O. Box 264-00606
  Sarit Centre, Nairobi, Kenya.

If you're a member of a book-club or would like to know more about how to form one, or seek ideas to lead a discussion of this book, others in the Storymoja series, or any book at all, please e-mail: ***bookclub@storymojaafrica.com.*** If you'd like to invite one of our authors to visit your school, book-club or other gathering, please e-mail ***invitation@storymojaafrica.com***

Fellow writers, we want to see your work

If your manuscript is hot enough to be selected for publication, we will provide an advance, help you edit, and guarantee you 20% royalties from sales. We may also invite you to attend our writer's workshops, so be sure to include your name, current address, telephone number and some information about yourself.

E-mail manuscript to: ***submissions@storymojaafrica.com***

Business books

We seek down-to-earth writing that deals with doing business in East Africa, writing that takes into consideration the local environment and regulatory conditions, writing about local industry that quotes local stakeholders. We're interested in business-related topics such as investment opportunities in Kenya or East Africa, entrepreneurial skills, stock market 101, business planning, sourcing finance, marketing, etc. Maximum length 10,000 words. Send us a sample of your writing and an outline of how you'd tackle a particular topic and we may commission you to write it.

Fiction

If you have a riveting work of fiction of about 12,000 words that you'd like us to consider for publication, e-mail, e-mail. We prefer work of East African identity that reflects the way we live today, whether the story is based here or abroad.

Life Changing Moments

Is there an event in your life that profoundly affected you? Perhaps it is a story of something that made you grow up real fast, or changed the way you do things, or altered the way you work or influenced how you deal with your family or other relationships, or an event that simply changed your perspective in a positive and meaningful way? Please share it with us in 2,000 words or less.

Humour

If you have a funny take on life, be it about the dating scene, or tribal stereotypes, or gender wars, or sports, in fact, on any aspect of living in our outrageous, hilarious, wonderful region, please send it in. Maximum length 10,000 words - but it could be in the form of a collection of shorter pieces. Bring tears of laughter to our eyes and we'll publish you.

True Crime Stories

Have you been conned? Cheated out of your property by relatives, friends, employees or strangers? Have you been mistreated, unjustly treated, mishandled, scammed, hijacked, carjacked, robbed or beaten? Do know of a scandal in your workplace? Are you the victim of a crime? We are looking for true crime stories and scandalous sagas of up to 10,000 words. And we'll protect your identity if you choose to remain anonymous in the publication. Outrage us and we'll publish you.

A taster from a Storymoja book of fiction; excerpts from Muthoni Garland's, *Tracking the Scent of My Mother*

'Afterwards, I'd climb the steepest part of the bank and clamber onto the rickety plank-and-rope bridge. Planting my bare buttocks on the planks, I'd dangle my feet over the edge, and dry in the sweet morning sun. It was on this very same plank-and-rope bridge, two years later, that I pushed my half-sister Faith into Ragati's rushing waters. It was not my fault that she had never learnt to swim.'

'Tracking the scent of my mother, I criss-crossed the streets of Karatina, but no-one claimed to have seen her. I described her, layer upon layer, like the topographical contours I'd later cover in school. Forming the words caused me pain because it forced me to see her as another, separate and different from me. I said, "My mother is tall. Her skin is the tender yellow of mashed cooking bananas, and her lips are tinged with pink. She has big breasts and hips and buttocks, but when she tightens her belt, her waist is narrow. Muscles bunch up in her calves like isolated potatoes, yet her legs are slender. Unlike Cousin Wangui, my mother's voice trips over certain letters, but it is deep and rare. My mother only wears shoes on Sundays. Her hair is in the latest curly kit fashion. She likes beads and bangles, and the itchy music of Congo . Western music makes her cry."'

> *As she grows from a child into a woman, Scholastica is confronted time and again by adversity. Bloodied but never bowed, she ploughs through her torments, believing that her confusion and loneliness will only cease once she is reunited with her mother. But as her life hurtles from one tragedy to another, culminating in a crime from which she surely cannot be saved, Scholastica's search never ends. Darkly comical and subtly explicit,* **Tracking the Scent of my Mother** *is an utterly believable work of fiction. Engaging, poetic, mesmerizing and masterfully told.*
>
> *Abdu Simba – Tanzanian Filmmaker*

A taster from a Storymoja inspirational anthology, *Life Changing Moments*; excerpt from Paul Ohaga's life changing experience.

'When you see an alien be careful. When you don't see one be even more careful. This has been my policy and stand when it comes to women. When I see one I like, I am careful. When I do not see any, I am extra careful. My story is not anything out of this world but it might be of help to you so read on.

My previous girlfriend had alleged that she was going to further her studies and left for the USA. What she really intended was to join her fiancé whom she had comfortably fooled me into believing was her cousin. But that is a story for another day. Suffice to say that at the hands of women I had suffered a series of heartbreaks and torment that reduced my once happy life to one of sorrow and regret.

That is, until a young Muslim woman came into my life. I had always yearned for a Muslim friend because nothing good had come of dating Christians. I imagined that because of their strict upbringing, Muslims, particularly women, were more honest and not as cruel when it came to matters of the heart.'